MINISTERO
PER I BENI E
LE ATTIVITÀ
CULTURALI

Maria Grazia Bernardini

Castel Sant'Angelo
National Museum

BRIEF ARTISTIC AND HISTORICAL GUIDE

«L'ERMA» di BRETSCHNEIDER

English translation
Oona Smyth for Scriptum, Rome

© Copyright 2012 «L'ERMA» di BRETSCHNEIDER
Via Cassiodoro, 19 - 00193 Roma
www.lerma.it - lerma@lerma.it

ISBN 978-88-8265-728-4

Contents

Foreword

This *Brief artistic and historical guide* published by the Superintendence for the Historic, Artistic and Ethno-Anthropological Heritage and for the Museum Group of the City of Rome, is intended to offer the many visitors to the National Museum of Castel Sant'Angelo a slim useful guide that will help them get to know this monument and its collection, steering them away from that devastating principle of "hit and run" tourism towards an in-depth visit of the site and inspiring them to seek a greater understanding of the past while, at the same time, discovering a new way of approaching it.

And visitors in search of the past will certainly find that Castel Sant'Angelo has a long and interesting story to tell. It begins with its celebrated origins as a mausoleum for Emperor Hadrian and his family and continues with the transformations that took place under the popes who turned it into an impregnable fortress and then into a sumptuous residence; it also touches upon the religious meaning linked to the appearance of the Archangel Michael on the summit of the building that ended the plague as well as to the pilgrim routes leading to St Peter's Basilica, and the building's use as a barracks and prison in Napoleonic times and at the very beginning of Italian unification followed by the establishment of the museum in 1925.

The *Brief artistic and historical guide*, written with elegance and expertise by Maria Grazia Bernardini, the museum's director, accompanies the public on this voyage of discovery, taking visitors by the hand as they embark upon different routes to explore the monument and its collections; the handy layouts are designed to allow visitors to personalize their visit at will and create their own unique in-depth experience.

The guide, which uses the new graphic layout adopted by the Superintendence, is the first in a new series that has been created to illustrate the museums and monuments managed by the board. We hope it will have the success it deserves and wish the visitors using it an enjoyable journey through a story mingling both past and present.

Rossella Vodret
Superintendent for the Historic, Artistic and Ethno-Anthropological Heritage
and for the Museum Group of the City of Rome

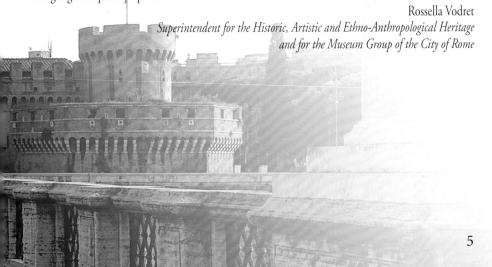

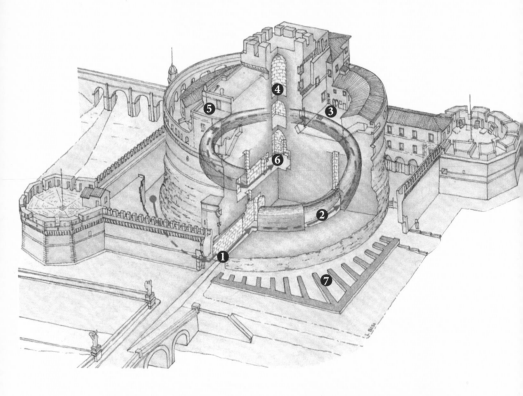

1. *Dromos*

2. *The Spiral Ramp*

3. *Courtyard of Alexander VI*

4. *The Treasury Chamber*

5. *Courtyard of the Angel*

6. *Chamber of the Urns*

7. *The Radial cells and the Staircase of Paul III*

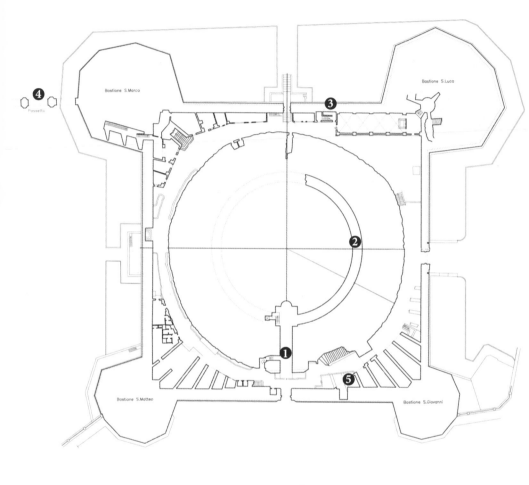

Bastione S.Marco

Bastione S.Luca

Passetto

Bastione S.Matteo

Bastione S.Giovanni

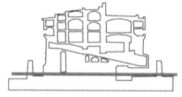

1. *Dromos*

2. *The Spiral Ramp*

3. *The Marcia Ronda*

4. *The Passetto di Borgo*

5. *The radial cells and the Staircase of Paul III*

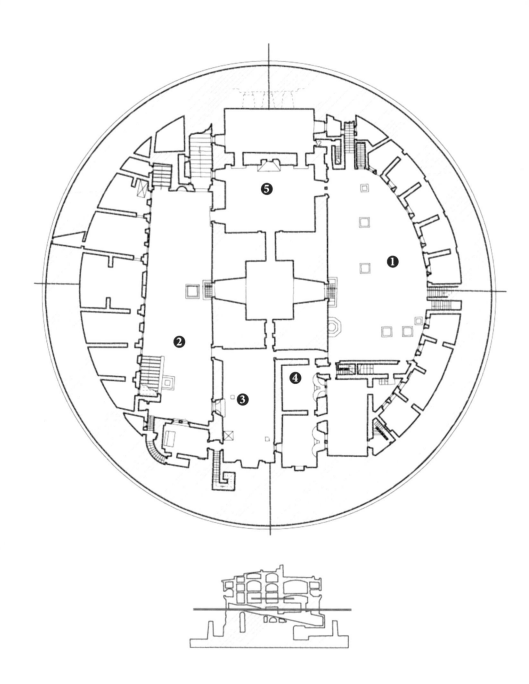

1. *Courtyard of Alexander VI*

2. *Courtyard of the Angel*

3. *Hall of Apollo*

4. *Room of Clemente VII, detail of frieze*

5. *Room of Clemente VIII*

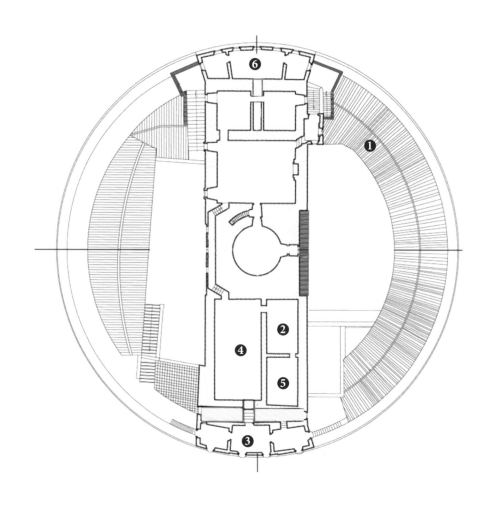

1. *Walkway of Pio IV*

2. *Perseus Room*

3. *Loggia of Julius II*

4. *The Pauline Hall*

5. *Love and Psyche Room*

6. *Loggia of Paul III*

National Museum of Castel Sant'Angelo

Castel Sant'Angelo is one of Rome's most iconic monuments. Its strategic location and over a thousand years of history have placed it at the heart of the city's life. Majestic mausoleum evoking the grandeur of the Roman empire, defensive citadel against barbarians or rioters, the magnificent abode and fortress of popes, dark and gloomy prison, and ideal setting for operas.

Today's castle is the result of extensive rebuilding and additions that have profoundly transformed its shape and original structure, making it difficult to comprehend a layout that is further obscured by a maze of rooms, ramps, corridors, courtyards, terraces, stairways, echoing halls and small chambers, and chapels. This labyrinth-like interior is part of what makes Castel Sant'Angelo so fascinating: the visit goes from the evocative ramp formerly used for funeral processions to Renaissance courtyards, from bleak prisons to splendid frescoed halls, and from the depths of the sepulchral cella to the roof terrace with its splendid vista of Rome.

The history of the monument

Publius Aelius Hadrianus, Trajan's adopted son, was Roman emperor from 117 to 138: erudite and noble, strong and austere, a valiant soldier as well as a shrewd politician, Hadrian was a lover of art, painting, music, philosophy and literature, and the period of his rule is considered one of the gold ages in the history of the Roman empire. The mausoleum that he built for himself and his family resembled the nearby tomb of Augustus, whose remains of which can be admired in Piazza Augusto Imperatore. The site where Hadrian decided to build his magnificent tomb was an isolated spot by the *ager Vaticanus*, on the far bank of the Tiber, outside the heart of the city. A bridge, the Pons Aelius, was built at the same time as the monument, linking the site to the city and making its isolation a purely logistical factor. Over the years the tomb was extensively transformed, adapted and defaced, making it impossible to reconstruct its original appearance, in particular, the part above the cylinder. Historic sources show that the tomb was built on three levels consisting of two superimposed cylindrical structures standing on a square base surrounded by a bronze enclosure. The external walls of the base, which was approximately 15m high, were clad in marble panels separated by pilaster strips and decorated with friezes, some fragments of which are on display in the rooms of the museum; bronze statues, possibly imported from Greece, stood on its four corners. The large cylindrical structure, which was also faced with travertine overlaid with marble, was surmounted by a series of statues that were destroyed over the centuries and an earthern tumulus planted with trees. In the centre stood a small temple, the cella holding the remains of the emperor, which bore a quadriga.

The mausoleum was joined to the city by the Pons Aelius, a bridge richly decorated with statues that was built for Hadrian. It was used as an imperial tomb for many years and it is said that the last emperor to be buried there was Caracalla in 217.

From the time of Aurelian onwards (271) it underwent extensive and complex transformations, as well as acts of vandalism that stripped the great mausoleum of all its bronze and marble decorations. Aurelian included the monument in the 19-km long walls built to defend his city from barbarian invasions, transforming it into a impregnable fortress by adding battlements with slits and crenellations to the square base and building walls that joined the parapets to the bridge.

In the 4th century, during the papacy of Pope Sylvester, Constantine built St Peter's Basilica on the site of the apostle's martyrdom, not far from Hadrian's tomb, drawing a flow of pilgrims to the area and causing a hamlet to spring up in the vicinity. It became known as the "Leonine citadel" after Pope Leo IV (852) had the settlement surrounded by defensive walls in response to a series of attacks.

The first phase of major rebuilding took place under Boniface IX (1389-1404): the cella on the top was reinforced and turned into a square tower, a ditch was dug around the cylindrical structure and the terrace on top of the square base was demolished to make the inner ward even more inaccessible.

The appearance of the monument was radically transformed during a second phase of work that took place under Nicholas V (1447-55), involving the construction of four bastions at the corner of the complex and a papal residence of modest dimensions on top of the cylinder abutting the central tower. This project was part of an extensive town-planning scheme involving the construction of high walls that would transform the Borgo district into a "papal citadel". The work begun by Nicholas V was completed under Alexander VI who surrounded the towers by bastions and built a tower in front of the bridge, joined the two front bastions by means of a high wall and dug an additional ditch around the entire complex, rebuilt the Passetto, or walkway joining the fortress to the Vatican, added crenellations to the top of the cylinder and enlarged the papal residence in the upper part of the castle.

The complex was by now an extraordinary fortress: Pope Paul III devoted himself to transforming it into a magnificent residence, building a second apartment that extended from the *Loggia of Julius II* to the other side of the terrace, where a second loggia was added, the *Loggia of Paul III*, and calling upon the leading artists of the time to decorate it with stuccoes and frescoes. The popes in the fol-

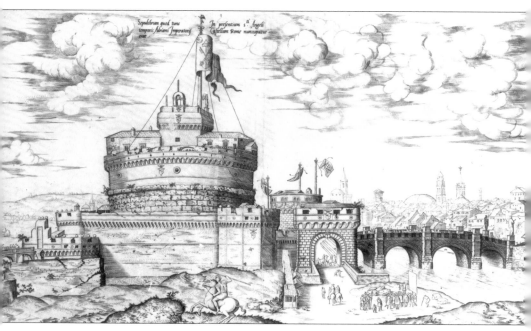

Master of the Bird's Wing (active in Rome 1546–1553). *Side view of Castel Sant'Angelo, burin engraving (copy after Enea Vico)*

Johann Wilhelm Stör (Nuremberg, active 1727–1755). *Reconstruction of Hadrian's Mausoleum and the Elio bridge (after J.B Fischer von Erlach, Entwurff einer Historischen Architectur, Vienna 1721)*

lowing centuries made only minimal changes, meaning that Castel Sant'Angelo had by now acquired its definitive appearance, although several major works were carried out on the exterior. For example, Pius IV erected pentagonal ramparts with five bastions extending to the rear of the building in a star-shaped layout, while Urban VIII had the tower by the bridge demolished and the entire area in front of the castle re-arranged. In 1699, Pope Clement IX had the bridge refurbished and decorated with statues by Giovan Lorenzo Bernini.

In 1870 the monument became the property of the Italian State and was used as a barracks and military prison. It was not until 1925, after the establishment of the museum, that the work of restoration began, works and collections were purchased and rooms were converted into exhibition spaces.

Emperor Hadrian's mausoleum
the Roman cylinder, dromos, spiral ramp and Chamber of the Urns

Roman cylinder

As visitors enter the museum they are immediately met by an imposing **cylinder** 64m in diameter and approximately 21m high; the core of Hadrian's sepulchre, its majesty can be admired from the *Ambulatory of Boniface IX* and the *Marcia Ronda*, the wall-walk running round the ramparts joining the four bastions. This tower, which represents the second level of the mausoleum, was formerly faced with travertine and marble slabs that have been destroyed over the centuries. Alexander VI (1492-1503) had it crowned with a high parapet on a series of small brick arches resting on top of marble corbels, which represented one of the most important additions. The façade bears a huge papal coat and arms flanked by figures of "Hunger" that was chiselled away by Napoleonic troops in 1798.

The main itinerary starts at the **dromos,** the entrance to the imperial tomb. Iron stairs lead to the atrium displaying a model showing a hypothetical reconstruction of the mausoleum on the left; the niche at the end formerly held a colossal statue of Hadrian, now in the Vatican Museum. On the right is the long **spiral ramp** formerly used by the funeral processions, which gently rises to the upper level, making a complete turn, and is diametrically crossed by the another ramp, named **diametrical ramp**, leading to the *Chamber of the Urns*. The floor of the ramp

Dromos

two side walls have two large arched niches and two slanted openings admitting light. Today the loss of the marble veneer and the addition of the bridge crossing the space make it hard to imagine the former splendour of this room. The *Chamber* is situated exactly at the centre of the mausoleum; above it, on the upper levels, are the *Hall of Justice*, the *Treasury* and the *Round Hall*.

The itinerary continues along the ramp to the *Courtyard of the Angel*.

The Spiral Ramp

still has traces of the ancient mosaic decoration while the walls, probably once clad with marble veneer, are made of skilfully laid brickwork. The vaulted ceiling, which may once have been decorated with stuccoes, has a series of air shafts, the last one of which bears a sign identifying it, probably wrongly, as the prison of San Marocco or Sammalo. Halfway along the ramp is the lofty sepulchral cella known as the **Chamber of the Urns,** which has a 10m-high ceiling. The rear wall and

Courtyard of the Angel

The *spiral ramp* and *diametrical ramp* lead to the **Courtyard of the Angel**, so named after the statue of Archangel Michael by the famous sculptor Raffaello di Montelupo, a pupil of Michelangelo (c. 1545). The sculpture originally stood on the top of the castle before being replaced by today's bronze statue in the 18th century (1752). This courtyard was formerly known as the *Courtyard of Honour* because it was overlooked by the papal apartments built under Nicholas V (1447-

Courtyard of the Angel

55). In the Middle Ages this courtyard joined the *Courtyard of Alexander VI* forming the summit of the Mausoleum, which was planted with a funerary garden until the apartments were built onto the central tower. On the right side of the *Courtyard of the Angel* is a two-storey medieval building while to the rear is the marble façade of the *Chapel of Leo X*, which was built by Michelangelo in 1514-15 and refurbished by Raffaello da Montelupo who was commissioned to restore the *courtyard* by Pope Paul III. Raffaello da Montelupo built a façade with a wall in which there was an oval niche holding a *Male portrait bust* by Guglielmo della Porta. Further along, on the left-hand side of the courtyard, is the huge façade of the two-storey papal apartments abutting the central tower. Two doorways lead to the ground floor, which was built in the 15th century under Nicholas V (and restored on several occasions by later popes), separating the two courtyards. This floor comprises the *Rooms of Clement VIII* and the *Hall of Justice*, the *Hall of Apollo* and *Rooms of Clement VII*. Among the famous prisoners standing trial in the *Hall of Justice* were Benvenuto Cellini and Beatrice Cenci.

The fourth wall, the one behind visitors as they leave the *diametrical ramp*, was re-arranged to resemble the rear wall by Raffaello da Montelupo who opened up two archways and an oval niche with a marble bust just like the one in the Chapel wall.

St Michael the Archangel

Hall of Apollo, Rooms of Clement VII and Chapel of Leo X

T he *Courtyard of the Angel* leads to the rooms built for Nicholas V (who converted the humble medieval dwelling built onto the tower into a modest apartment where he could take refuge in case of danger) and decorated under Popes Clement VII, Paul III and Clement VIII.

The **Hall of Apollo**, one of the finest rooms in the Museum of Castel Sant'Angelo, has an elaborate ceiling comprising a shallow barrel vault and pendentives emblazoned with the papal arms in the central oval; the spacious room is decorated throughout with elegant grotesques depicting dancers, musicians, centaurs fighting, playful putti and other mythological figures as well as a series of scenes illustrating the myth of Apollo. The god of sun and beauty, music and poetry, Apollo symbolizes the golden age; at the same time he is a fierce dangerous god representing moral order. The frescoes were commissioned from Perin del Vaga but executed by Domenico Rietti, Lo Zaga, in 1547-48.

Hall of Apollo

Hall of Apollo (detail)

Like several other rooms in Castel Sant'Angelo including the *Hall of the Library*, the *Pompeian-style corridor* and various rooms in the Farnese apartment, the *Hall of Apollo* documents the popularity of the "grotesque" genre following the rediscovery of the *Domus Aurea* by pupils of Raphael, Giovanni da Udine and Perin del Vaga.

The *Hall of Apollo* leads to a **chapel** dedicated to **Sts Cosmas and Damian**, which was redecorated by Michelangelo in 1514-16 during the period of Leo X. The involvement of this outstanding artist is confirmed by a series of drawings and a sheet held by the Musèe des Beaux Arts of Lille stating "questo in chastello in Roma di mano di Michelagnolo di traverti…".

The visit continues in the two **Rooms of Clement VII**, which have friezes executed by Bartolomeo Griechi and Matteo Crassetti in 1533 (probably after drawings by Giulio Romano) that run below the lovely wooden ceilings: the first room has intriguing frescoes featuring acanthus spirals and putti holding cartouches with inscriptions referring to the pope.

After going back to the *Hall of Apollo*, visitors can choose between entering the *Courtyard of Alexander VI* or continuing through the papal apartments with the *Hall of Justice* and the *Rooms of Clement VIII*.

23

Courtyard of Alexander VI

Also known as the ***Courtyard of the Crossbow*** after the ancient crossbow that has stood here for many years or, more correctly, the *Courtyard of the Theatre* for the theatrical performances held here in the time of Leo X, this is a delightful site enclosed by a curved façade on one side and featuring an attractive wellhead bearing the coat of arms of Alexander VI where the castle's inhabitants once drew their water. The façade of the building, which was refurbished under the Borgias, is decorated with painted friezes and mythological scenes, unfortunately in very poor condition, between the windows and doors leading to the upper floor (*Pius IV's walkway*), to the rooms or to the famous **Prisons** and **Oil Stores** (although normally closed, these rooms can be visited by requesting a guided tour).

Below the courtyard are a series of rooms that were carved out of the semi-circular wall enclosing Hadrian's tomb and used as storerooms for wheat, oil and water from the Tiber, which was filtered through three cisterns, as well as prisons. After passing the *Parlour* the stairs lead to a low-ceilinged corridor flanked by a series of dark gloomy cells followed by the silos. From Renaissance times until the 19th century these cells were prisons whose occupants numbered the like of Pope Paul III, the Italian Humanist Pomponio Leto, Benvenuto Cellini, Giordano Bruno, Beatrice Cenci, and Count Cagliostro. One of the most tragic tales concerned Beatrice Cenci, a young Roman noblewoman who lived in the late 16th century. To put an end to her father's abuse, she had him murdered. Despite the moral justification for her actions, she was sentenced to death and executed on Sant'Angelo Bridge before a huge crowd that was moved by her cruel fate.

Stufetta of Clement VII and Courtyard of Leo X

Stufetta of Clement VII (detail)

A passageway to the rear of the *Courtyard of Alexander VI* leads to the delightful *Bathroom of Clement VII* and the *Courtyard of Leo X*, which are normally closed but can be visited by requesting a guided tour.

The ***Stufetta (bathroom) of Clement VII***, a jewel of mid-16th-century architectural and decorative art, is named after the pope who had it completed. The complex comprises a small bathroom, a room below where the water was heated up and an upper room used as the pope's changing room. Almost every surface of the tiny bathroom (260 x 150 cm) was decorated by Giovanni da Udine (probably using designs by Giulio Romano) with stuccoes and grotesque-style frescoes featuring putti, dolphins, swans, plant motifs, mythological scenes and the thrones of the Olympian gods who have put down their attributes and draped their garments over them in order to accompany the pope in his ablutions.

The Castel Sant'Angelo *Bathroom* is one of the few surviving Renaissance bathrooms. The Italian name *Stufetta*, or bathhouse, evokes the concept of therapeutic Roman steam baths. The water heating system is still visible today and consists of a narrow channel running around the edge of the floor, three pipes in the wall and a small back room.

The ***Courtyard of Leo X***, which dates to the 15th-century refurbishments completed under this Medici pope, originally had a delightful roof garden where the popes could wile away their time.

Stufetta of Clement VII

Walkway of Pius IV

The Barberini bees on the balustrade globes indicate that the staircase at the rear of the *Courtyard of the Angel* leading up to the *Loggia of Julius II* was built under Urban VIII. After passing a small staircase leading to the *Sala Paolina* on the left, it reaches the *Walkway of Pius IV*, which is the corridor running along the outside walls. The neighbouring rooms are part of a building overlooking the *Courtyard of Alexander VI*. Originally used as munitions deposit, they were later transformed into "VIP" prisons. This first section of the gallery, which has glazed openings, holds a display of stone fragments, heads, cornices, friezes, reliefs with lion protomes and capitals that were part of the decorations of the ancient mausoleum. Here visitors can take the stairs leading down to the *Courtyard of Alexander VI* or continue to the *Loggia of Paul III* and *Hall of the Library*. Proceeding along the gallery, there is a café where they can enjoy one of the most spectacular views of Rome before returning to the point of departure.

Walkway of Pius IV

The Pauline Hall, Pompeian-style corridor and Loggia of Julius II

The *Pauline Hall* is the most magnificent room in the entire complex, and its stucco and fresco decorative scheme is one of the most significant artistic accomplishments of mid-16th-century Rome.

Paul III was elected pope in 1534 at a particularly difficult and complex moment in history: the aftermath of the Sack of Rome of 1527 was very much present, Martin Luther's teachings were making waves throughout Europe, heresies were rife, and engravings and texts attacking the Catholic Church were widespread. Aware of the need for a strong hand at the helm of the Church and for measures tackling the heresies, on the one hand, and for much-needed reforms of the ecclesiastic bodies on the other, the pope launched an incredible series of political, administrative, social and cultural initiatives, including a vast programme of artistic and urban renewal in Rome, the new

The Pauline Hall, detail of allegorical females figures

The Pauline Hall

Jerusalem and supreme centre of the Christian community.

He had the papal apartments at Castel Sant'Angelo extended and decorated, adding a floor on top of the rooms built for Nicholas V. This second storey, which extends from the *Loggia of Julius II* overlooking the Tiber to the *Loggia of Paul III* overlooking the meadows below, is composed of a series of magnificently decorated rooms: the *Pauline Hall*, the *Camera di Amore e Psiche* and the *Perseus Room*, the *Pompeian-style corridor* leading to the *Hadrianeum* and the *Room of Festoons*. For good reason the Latin inscription running below the cornice of all four walls of the *Pauline Hall* reads: "Those things which in this fortress were once collapsed, useless and ruined are now by Paul III, Pontifex Maximus, in strong solidity, comfortable usefulness and refined beauty conspicuously replaced, restored and decorated".

The dense decorations of the *Pauline Hall* cover both walls and ceil-

Pompeian-style corridor

ings with episodes from the lives of Alexander the Great and St Paul that clearly allude to the pope whose birth name was Alessandro Farnese and who took the name Paul when he was raised to the See of Rome. The six frescoed ceiling panels depicting episodes from the life of Alexander the Great are enclosed by sumptuous gilded and white stucco decorations, while on the walls the fresco decorations come to the fore and even the columns separating the scenes are painted. The end walls are dominated by the figures of Archangel Michael and Emperor Hadrian who symbolize both the location and the Roman and Christian cultures that followed each other, becoming indissolubly bound together: the long side walls have large monochrome panels imitating bronze that depict episodes from the life of Alexander the Great while the small medallions over the doors showing scenes from the life of St Paul are held up by allegorical figures symbolising the Virtues who are seated on the cornices. Fights between marine creatures are painted in the socle. The entire iconographic scheme is designed to exalt the Farnese family and the concept of the papacy as an expression of universal power that reigns supreme, even over emperors.

Loggia of Julius II

The decorations were executed in 1545-47 after being entrusted to Perin del Vaga, the leading heir of the school of Raphael and one of the favourite artists of the pope who appointed him court painter. Following in the footsteps of his great master, Perin del Vaga set up an extremely active workshop, which allowed him to carry out his numerous commissions; several of his pupils worked with him on the *Pauline Hall* including Marco Pino who painted the ceiling frescoes, Domenico Zaga, Siciolante da Sermoneta, Pellegrino Tibaldi and, possibly, Livio Agresti.

Moving away from the harmonious classicizing style of the High Renaissance that represented the great achievement of the early 16th century, Perin and his helpers gave birth to a powerful display of the "maniera" style that had emerged towards the middle of the century thanks to both his art and that of Francesco Salviati and Daniele da Volterra, the two other protagonists of the Farnese era. Although deeply rooted in classical art, Perin's language adopted elegant precious forms aiming at highly decorative effects. He eschewed vast scenes occupying entire walls like the Michelangelo and Raphael's frescoes for scenes enclosed in clearly defined frames separated by lush ornamental elements. The sopraporta decorations feature tondos with episodes from the life of St Paul that are held up by slender elegant allegorical figures accompanied by putti, festoons and other objects in an abundance of motifs distracting attention from the main theme and forming a lively dynamic visual composition.

Love and Psyche Room, Perseus Room

The two small rooms adjoining the large Pauline Hall, and currently being prepared as an exhibition space, are the private rooms of the pope; they led directly via a small staircase to the *Stufetta of Clement VII*, and to the two adjacent courtyards, the *Courtyard of Alexander VI* and the *Courtyard of Leo X*.

The **Love and Psyche Room** has a beautiful frescoed frieze executed by Perin del Vaga and his assistants in 1545-46, which depicts the story of Psyche as told by Apuleius in the *Golden Ass*. Psyche is a young girl whose beauty arouses the envy of Venus. The goddess decides to get her revenge by asking her son Cupid to use his arrows to make Psyche fall in love with a man of low birth, but little does she imagine that Cupid himself will fall head over heels in love with the girl. Cupid takes Psyche to his palace where he pays her nightly visits, ensuring that she never catches sight of his face. One night Psyche's curi-

Love and Psyche Room

Love and Psyche Room, detail of frieze

Love and Psyche Room, detail of frieze

osity gets the better of her and, lamp in hand, she pulls back the sheets to reveal her youthful lover. A drop of hot oil falls from the lamp onto Cupid's bare skin, waking him and causing him to flee in disappointment. Psyche sets off on a desperate search for Cupid, ending up at the palace of Venus who uses the occasion to punish her by setting her a series of terrible tasks. However, Psyche manages to carry them all out and Cupid takes her to Olympus to be his bride.

Psyche in Greek means breath, soul, life, or butterfly, and the complexity of the story means that this myth can be interpreted on many levels. In this context the choice of theme probably alludes to the arduous journey that the human soul must make before being purified, a clear reference to the difficulties being experienced at the time by the papacy, which was suffering from corruption and immoral behaviour.

Perseus Room, detail of frieze

The **Perseus Room**, originally a *studiolo*, is decorated with a larger frieze composed of six panels alternating with pairs of allegorical figures with a unicorn, the emblem of the Farnese family, surrounded by putti in the myth of the Greek hero narrated in Ovid's *Metamorphoses*. The story unfolds from left to right, with scenes showing *Perseus Taking Leave of his mother Danae and Polydectes, Perseus with Mercury and Minerva, the Killing of the Medusa, the Return of Perseus, the Origin of Coral* and *the Wedding of Perseus and Andromeda*. The story of Perseus, the son of Jupiter and Danae, the sun-like god who fought the power of darkness and struggled to overcome terrifying difficult tasks like killing the Medusa and freeing Andromeda, probably alludes to the battle of Paul III against Lutheran reform and the heresies spreading through Europe like wildfire. This frieze was also executed by Perin del Vaga with the collaboration of his helpers led by Domenica Zaga, who was to take charge of work after the death of his master. The decorations in this room show how Perin's iconographic approach evolved from the continuous frieze on view in the *Rooms of Clement VII* to these small panels separated by large allegorical figures.

These two rooms intended for private use by Paul III draw upon mythology and fable, and a rich ornamental style of painting sharing the same religious meanings but quite unlike the official genre of painting epitomized in Michelangelo's *Last Judgement* for the Sistine Chapel, unveiled only a few years before (1541) and commissioned by the same pope.

Library and Loggia of Paul III

The vast chamber formerly known as the "sala nova verso Prata" (new hall overlooking what is now the Prati district) and which probably takes its current name from the presence of documents of the Papal States is situated on the opposite side of the complex to the *Pauline Hall* and can be reached via the *Pompeian-style corridor* from the *Pauline Hall* or via the **Loggia of Paul III**, a loggia with five arches built by Raffaello da Montelupo and frescoed with scenes from the life of Emperor Hadrian by Siciolante da Sermoneta. The *Library* was the first room to be entrusted to Perin del Vaga's pupil Luzio Luzi, who decorated it in 1544-45 with a rich decorative scheme of frescoes and stuccoes in the manner developed by Raphael and his pupils - in particular Giovanni da Udine; this model, first used in the Vatican Loggias and in Villa Madama, was based on a profound knowledge of Roman art and classicial culture in general, and was to enjoy great success and diffusion. The ceiling decorations feature Archangel Michael and Emperor Hadrian, scenes from the history of Rome, allegories of Pan and Daphne along with ornamental motifs and whimsical grotesques, and a lively festive frieze

Hall of the Library

with nereids and marine creatures. The walls have fragments of frescoes with the coats of arms and emblems of Pope Paul III and allegorical figures of the Church and Rome belonging to a programme exalting both the Farnese papacy and the Church.

The *Hall of the Library* leads to the **Treasury**, so called for the chests used to store the money and valuables of the Apostolic Chamber. According to a reconstruction carried out by scholars, Emperor Hadrian was laid to rest here. The cupboards are original furnishings dating to 1545.

Loggia of Paul III

The Treasury Chamber

Hadrianeum Room and Room of Festoons

The *Hall of the Library* leads to two adjoining rooms, the first known as the **Hadrianeum Room** for the hypothetical depiction of Hadrian's mausoleum in the painted frieze at the top of the wall and the second known as the **Room of Festoons** for the decorative motifs in the frescoes.

The frieze in the first room, which was probably executed by Prospero Fontana in 1544-45, depicts the triumphs of the nymphs Galatea and Ariadne, the discovery of wine, and Achilles with his mother Thetis. There is also an extremely interesting series of painted monuments between figures of Caryatids including the *Meta Romuli*, the *Naumachia*, the *Circus of Caligula* and *Hadrian's Mausoleum*.

The second room has a lovely frieze with a woman and unicorn, one of the emblems of Pope Paul III, a symbol exalting chastity that has obvious religious implications.

The Hadrianeum Room

The Angel

High up on the top of the fortress is the figure of Archangel Michael, the symbol of the monument, recalling a miraculous event of 590, the year in which a terrible plague was devastating Rome. As Pope Gregory the Great led a procession pleading for God's intercession, the Archangel Michael appeared on the top of the mausoleum, sheathing his sword to indicate the end of the epidemic; and from the 7th century onwards, Hadrian's Mausoleum has been dedicated to this Archangel.

The presence of Archangel Michael, which gives a strong religious connotation to what was once a pagan monument, is probably what inspired Giovan Lorenzo Bernini's decorative scheme for the bridge. His sculptures of *Angels* holding the symbols of the Passion transformed the Pons Aelius, as it had been known ever since its inception as a triumphal entrance to Hadrian's mausoleum, into the Ponte Sant'Angelo, creating a spiritual journey for the pilgrims from the north travelling to St Peter's Basilica, the centre of Christianity.

The current bronze statue was made by the Flemish artist Pieter Verschaffelt and erected in 1752 to replace the marble sculpture by Raffaello di Montelupo that now stands in *Courtyard of the Angel*.

The Angel

Passetto di Borgo

The **Passetto di Borgo** is an evocative covered walkway approximately 800m long that runs along the top of the walls formerly bounding the Leonine citadel and links the castle to the Vatican palace. Built in part to facilitate the pope's access to his private apartments, its main function was to provide an escape route in case of danger. It was first used under Nicholas III (1277-80), then re-arranged un-

Passetto di Borgo

der Nicholas V who was responsible for the rebuilding of the Borgo district and the creation of papal apartments in the castle. The *Passetto* took on strategic importance during the Sack of Rome of 1527, allowing Clement VII to flee from the marauding Landsknechts.

Bastions and Marcia Ronda

As it descends, the ***Diametrical Ramp*** leading from the *Courtyard of the Angel* to the entrance is crossed by a drawbridge leading to the ***Marcia Ronda***. The sentries on guard duty would do their rounds along this wall-walk running along the outer curtain wall joining the four bastions. The first nucleus of the bastions was built for Nicholas V who gave orders for four large towers to be erected to defend the building from continuous attacks (only three were actually built). This project was part of a vast rebuilding plan concerning the entire Leonine city created by Leo IV between the fortress and the Vatican and surrounded by massive high walls that extended around the Vatican palaces.

Alexander VI took further steps to transform Hadrian's mausoleum into a fortress-like complex when he had Antonio da Sangallo the Younger build four mighty bastions joined by a curtain wall

The Bastion of St John

The Marcia Ronda

incorporating the towers built previously under Nicholas V.

Turning to the right visitors encounter the **Bastion of St Matthew,** the **Bastion of St Mark** followed by the **Bastion of St Luke** with its adjoining rectangular building formerly used as an armoury. On the ground-floor of this block is the *Chapel of the Crucifix,* which opens onto the *Courtyard of Execution,* where condemned criminals were executed by firing squad. The wall-walk continues to the **Bastion of St John**, which features a gunsmith's workshop reconstructed in the early 20th century, before reaching the *Staircase of Paul III* leading to the exit.

The National Museum of Castel Sant'Angelo and its collection

After becoming the property of the Italian State in 1870, the monument was used as a barracks and military prison. It was not until 1925 that it was transformed into a museum under legislation establishing that it was to hold works of historical and artistic interest, weapons and mementos of the Italian Army. For years the Museum collected and acquired important collections of weapons, medals, watercolours and uniforms, and an important group of weapons from Gradara castle, which represents the most important collection on display. It comprises an *arquebus* from the Farnese period, an Italian leather-covered *rotella*, or round parade shield, dating to the mid-16th century along with an iron *parade shield*, a 14th-century *great helm*, two splendid *pistols*, the uniform of *General Hermann Kanzler, commander of the papal troops,* and the 18th-century *standard of the Bombardieri di Castel Sant'Angelo.*

Arquebus Farnese

Part of this splendid collection is on display in the rooms opening onto the *Walkway of Pius IV* near the café.

The Museum also holds important stone artefacts, many of which belonging to the ancient decorations of Hadrian's Mausoleum, along with Renaissance sculptures, paintings from various periods, porcelain objects, engravings and drawings.

The castle gallery has two main collections: the Menotti collection, which was donated to the museum in 1916 to decorate the rooms of the apartment of Paul III, and the Contini Bonacossi collection, which was acquired in 1928. As well as paintings, this second group also includes furniture, chests, chairs and faldstools chosen to furnish the castle rooms in Renaissance style.

Among the paintings is a fine *Polyptych* by the workshop of the Zavattari, a group of painters active in Lombardy in the 15th century; two small panels by Carlo Crivelli depicting a *Blessing Christ* and *St Onuphrius*; a *St Jerome* painted by Lorenzo Lotto during his brief Roman stay in 1509; an altarpiece

Lorenzo Lotto, *San Girolamo*

Workshop of the Zavattari, *Polyptych*

depicting the *Virgin with Child and Saints* by Luca Signorelli dating to 1515-20, and the *Bacchanal* by Dosso Dossi. There is also a noteworthy *Portrait of a Young Woman with Unicorn* by Luca Longhi, dating to the second half of the 16th century. The lady with the unicorn is one of the emblems of the Farnese family, and the woman in the portrait has tentatively been identified as Giulia Farnese, the daughter of Pier Luigi Farnese and Giovannella Caetani. The Farnese family owed the success and power that it acquired in the 16th century to the charms of this young woman; with the Borgia pope, Alexander VI, at her feet, she was in a position to favour the rise of the Farnese family.

The entire museum is currently being refurbished and the collections are temporarily not on display. The re-display will involve the collection of weapons on show in the rooms by the Marcia Ronda, the paintings and sculptures in the papal apartments and the stone fragments in the so-called grottoni, *or radial cells on the ground floor to the right of the entrance.*

Who can forget the choice of Castel Sant'Angelo as the setting for the final act of Puccini's Tosca? Tosca goes to the castle to meet her beloved Mario Cavaradossi, a painter who had been working in the church of Sant'Andrea della Valle, hoping to free him after stabbing the hateful Scarpia. Realizing that she has been deceived and that Cavaradossi has been executed, the young woman flings herself to her death from the castle ramparts.

Notes

Notes

Notes